# Bright Interval

A play

Cherry Vooght

Samuel French—London
New York-Toronto-Hollywood

## CHARACTERS

**Kate,** a college lecturer, leader of the tour
**Frau Rosa Klein,** owner of the hotel, early middle age
**Lottie,** probably the youngest, has a son aged 14
**Freda,** ex-teacher, several years retired
**Elizabeth,** on her first tour, early middle age
**Flo,** tough, hard-working, respectable background, roughly
  the same age as Freda

Ages can be freely adaptable within the realm of credibility

## COPYRIGHT INFORMATION
(See also page ii)

## NOTE TO PRODUCERS

The mood of the play changes frequently as the characters come and go, and situations alter. The dialogue is sometimes light-hearted and often thoughtful and introspective. There are many pauses. Some are quite long, and it is important that these should be held. Conversation and behaviour should be easy and natural, never over-played.

The wine has a minimal effect of warming the atmosphere and stimulating ideas — but there must be no hint of alcohol-effect on any of the characters.

The setting should give considerable freedom and opportunity for the imagination of the producers and designers. It could be extremely simple or a stage picture full of colouful detail. A great deal of the presentation's atmosphere will depend on the skill of the electrician in making the relevant lighting changes.

Cherry Vooght

*Also by Cherry Vooght*
*published by Samuel French Ltd*

Barbecue
People Like Us

"Travel, in the younger sort, is a part of education;
in the elder, a part of experience."
*Essays* "Of Travel" (1625) by Francis Bacon

To Cliff

# BRIGHT INTERVAL

*The flower-decked terrace of a small family-run hotel in the Austrian Tyrol. It is late afternoon on a very warm summer day*

*The distant view from the terrace is towards a range of high snow-capped mountains. There is an untidy scattering of garden furniture — small tables; chairs; sun-loungers, etc. Some bottles of wine and glasses remain on one of the small tables — evidence of a recent party*

*When the* CURTAIN *rises, Kate is sprawled out on a sun-lounger chair beside the laden table. There is a full glass of wine beside her. She kicks off her shoes with some relief*

*Frau Rosa Klein, the hotel owner, enters and moves towards Kate. She is a smiling woman and is handsomely dressed in full Tyrolean costume*

**Frau Klein** Worn out?

**Kate** Sore feet. And the first chance I've had to enjoy a drink.

**Frau Klein** It seemed a very successful party.

**Kate** It was.

**Frau Klein** There's quite a lot of wine left.

**Kate** They opened too many bottles.

**Frau Klein** A variety of labels.

**Kate** A variety of tastes. Anton's choice — and he and Trudi set it up for us.

**Frau Klein** Good.

**Kate** Will you try this? I can recommend it.

**Frau Klein** Thank you — no. I need a clear head for your dinner tonight. The final meal must be special.

**Kate** Every meal here is special.

**Frau Klein** My hotel staff always look forward to your tours. You bring such appreciative guests.

**Kate** We're lucky. The college attracts such interesting people — all ages and backgrounds. By the way, I heard Trudi trying to explain our tour to a German guest. She described us as "people who hadn't learned much at school".

**Frau Klein** Oh dear. She forgets you speak German.

**Kate** I thought it was a nice summing-up of adult education.

*Frau Klein takes a small, ornate parcel from her pocket*

**Frau Klein** I have a small souvenir for you.

**Kate** (*placing the parcel on the table*) Oh — how kind.

**Frau Klein** It's to open as you're leaving Austria. I know it's always sad for you.

**Kate** Emotional — every time. But once I'm a few miles away I look forward to being home again.

**Frau Klein** There's someone in your group who may feel as deeply as you. I expect you know …

**Kate** Elizabeth.

**Frau Klein** I had a long talk with her yesterday. Not much for her to go home to I imagine.

**Kate** No. A determined invalid of a mother.

**Frau Klein** Heaven's door has opened here for Elizabeth.

**Kate** Her first visit — and I know what that can mean. (*Pause*) What about you, Rosa? While we are here — or some other British tour — don't you ever feel you want to come back and live in England?

**Frau Klein** Never. Never — not even when Andreas died. To everyone here I am an Austrian widow. My life is here.

**Kate** How many others died in that terrible avalanche?

**Frau Klein** Forty-three; here and in St Anton.

**Kate** Aren't you ever afraid — now?

**Frau Klein** Aware — not afraid. It's a price you accept for living in the mountains. Now I'm going to leave you in peace. It's good for you to have a bit of time to yourself.

**Kate**  Please stay. We don't often have a chance to talk.

**Klein**  I suppose most people are busy packing. It's a very early start tomorrow.

**Kate**  A few have gone to St Anton. Bill and some others wanted to go to the woodcarver's again — so Harry is dropping them off before taking the coach to fill up with diesel. Bill has taken a fancy to an enormous angel he saw there last week.

**Klein**  For his church?

**Kate**  For his house.

**Klein**  Has he got such a big house?

**Kate**  An ordinary semi I believe.

**Klein**  Extraordinary. Anyway, would he get it past Customs?

**Kate**  Don't worry. He won't get it past Harry.

**Klein**  Harry is a gem, isn't he? Much more than a very good driver.

**Kate**  He's a diamond. He loves our tours — and he's a very important part of our organizing team, with Brian and me.

**Klein**  Has Brian gone to St Anton?

**Kate**  Yes, to help with any last-minute currency problems.

**Klein**  You spoil them.

*Lottie hurries in*

**Lottie**  (*with laughter in her voice*) Katie — be prepared for another Freda episode.

**Kate**  What now?

**Lottie**  Freda has lost her passport

**Kate**  Oh no!

*Freda enters slowly and out of breath*

**Lottie**  I've told Kate that you've lost your passport.

**Freda**  I have not lost my passport. I know where it is…

**Kate**  Well — where is it?

**Freda**  I must have posted it yesterday with my postcards.

**Kate**  Posted it?!

**Freda**  It was in my handbag.

**Kate**  You mean your passport is well on its way to England, and you are still in Austria!

**Freda**  That's right.

**Kate**  No, Freda — that is not right. To get home you have to cross three frontiers and go through Customs at Calais and Dover.

**Lottie**  Never mind, Freda. You'll just have to stay here until they can post it back.

**Freda**  Oh, no! It's my grandaughter's wedding on Saturday.

**Lottie**  Freda, dear — the Customs' gentlemen will not be moved by your family problems.

**Klein**  Don't worry — it's happened before, so we can help you. You'll need to get a certificate from the police. It's rather a fuss, but I'm sure Anton will go with you to the *polizei* — to make it easier for you.

**Freda**  How awful. Those grey men with guns?

**Klein**  They're not as fierce as they look. But they will ask you a lot of personal questions.

**Freda**  Oh, Lord.

**Klein**  The police office doesn't open again until six o'clock — but please come with me now and we'll speak to Anton.

**Kate**  Had I better come?

**Klein**  No need. Stay and rest your feet for the journey tomorrow — up and down the coach. They tell me you walked to Austria.

**Freda**  I'd like Flo to come with us. Will that be all right?

**Klein**  By all means.

**Freda**  I'll go and find her.

**Klein**  Anton first — while he's still in the bar …

*Frau Klein and Freda exit*

**Lottie**  Freda and Flo; I feel sorry for the police.

**Kate**  Lottie, I forbid you to tease Freda.

**Lottie**  It's so tempting — she does ask for it, doesn't she? I don't think we've visited a café or shop in France or Germany or Austria that Freda believes has given her the right change. In Italy she nearly got us run in by the Mafia.

**Kate**  She gets confused. Currency is not her strong point.

**Lottie**  Neither is packing. Without help she'd still be at our first overnight. I know more about Freda's knickers than she does.

**Kate** You've been very good to her.

**Lottie** It's more bearable with a bit of teasing. She's got this huge case on wheels — like a truck, and just as heavy. Poor Harry has had to heave it into the luggage boot every time. It's probably ruined his family life.

**Kate** Will you have some left-over wine?

**Lottie** Love some. (*She sits comfortably*)

*Kate pours Lottie a glass of wine and hands it to her*

Did you see the notice in that café last week? "Our wines leave you nothing to hope for".

**Kate** Liz took a picture of it.

**Lottie** What a glorious place! If we could all live in scenery like this, I'm sure we'd be kind, good people living in an ideal world.

**Kate** I doubt it. Hitler lived in Berchtesgarten.

**Lottie** So he did. What a pity. I thought I'd found an answer.

**Kate** Someone is coming up the steps. A red dress. Oh, it's Elizabeth. Doesn't she look delightful?

**Lottie** She has style, that woman. (*She waves*) I saw her having a long chat with Rosa Klein. They seem to get on well.

*Elizabeth (Liz) enters. She has a small camera suspended from a chord around her neck*

*Lottie welcomes her*

Hallo, Liz.

**Liz** Hallo, Lottie. I hear that Freda has posted her passport. It can't be true.

**Lottie** It can for Freda.

**Liz** It was late to be sending cards, wasn't it?

**Lottie** Not for Freda. She wrote them the first day we got here, then forgot them. (*She offers Elizabeth some wine*) Left-over, but good.

**Liz** Lovely.

*Lottie pours a glass of wine for Liz*

I met Freda just now — looking for Flo. A strange friendship to begin here.

**Kate**  But so good. Two lonely people — which I suppose is not surprising.

**Liz**  It's hard to think of Freda as an ex-teacher.

**Kate**  She was a very good teacher — at a famous school for many years …

**Liz**  Until she retired?

**Kate**  Yes. Freda never got over the shock of retirement — and losing her husband a few months later. She can't get to terms with the practical day-to-day world — and getting old.

**Lottie**  I think getting old could be restful. An excuse to stop hankering after things you may not have enjoyed anyway.

**Liz**  It depends on how much you got out of being young. (*Pause, while she takes the wine*) I heard some loud singing as I passed David's door just now.

**Lottie**  That will be David and the *Messiah*. I wouldn't mind if he stopped the tape before that awful "Hallelujah Chorus" .

**Liz**  Your room is next door, isn't it?

**Lottie**  It's OK. I'm used to noise.

**Liz**  It was a splendid party, Kate. Everyone so beautifully mixed up — and talking their heads off.

**Kate**  That's why we have the party. It isn't easy to socialize in a coach, without severe bruising.

**Lottie**  Very true. Several of the coffee-making team were comparing bruises yesterday. Little did you all know how bravely we suffered. Abigail has a bruise on her thigh like the map of Africa. I'm off to meet her now, in the bar — yet another aperitif. Live dangerously while we can. Coming, Kate? Liz?

**Kate**  My legs prefer to live quietly — while they can.

**Liz**  I want to take one or two more photos.

**Lottie**  See you later at the feast. Final feast — alas!

*Lottie exits*

*The two women are quiet. Elizabeth moves away to take a picture of the mountains. It is clear that she is fighting tears*

**Kate** Your pictures will make a lovely souvenir, Liz.

*There is no reply from Elizabeth and Kate realizes she is crying. She goes to Elizabeth*

Liz — what's the matter, love?

**Liz** (*with difficulty through her tears*) I'm sorry, Kate. Please don't let me upset you … It's just — I can't bear to leave — all this.

**Kate** It's meant so much to you?

**Liz** Beyond anything words can deal with. The me who came to Austria no longer exists.

**Kate** In two weeks?

**Liz** In a few minutes; the first time I stepped on to this terrace. I was — overwhelmed. The impact was immediate — complete, and I knew I would never be the same again. It sounds so ridiculous.

**Kate** No. I think it happens to a lot of people. It happens to me every time I come back. And you'll be back too.

**Liz** Not easy. Certainly not for a long time. When I rang Laura — my sister — last night, it was obvious that she and Tony are counting the hours to bringing mother back.

**Kate** Is she very difficult?

**Liz** No. People find her quite charming.

**Kate** And you?

**Liz** Wearying — day after day. She refuses to try any kind of activity, so our world revolves around ailments and TV.

**Kate** Not a bright picture.

**Liz** It does lack sparkle. When I get home I must try to settle down again to the old routine.

**Kate** Must you?

**Liz** It's the monotony I can't take, the boredom. I feel I'm getting dull, dull, dull — taking more and more time to do less and less — or even nothing.

**Kate** You can still smile, Liz. People have remarked on Elizabeth's smile. Honest, it's true.

**Liz**  If it wasn't you'd make it up to cheer me.

**Kate**  Liz, I saw you reading a poetry book on the coach. Do you know the Fitzgerald version of "Omar Khayyám"?

**Liz**  Very well.

**Kate**  There's good advice for you — two lines.

> "Ah, fill the cup: — What boots it to repeat
> How time is slipping underneath our feet ...".

Think it over, Liz.

**Liz**  It's wishful thinking, Kate. Dear Kate, thank you for all that you and Brian have done to make these two weeks so memorable — for everyone.

**Kate**  Brian and I really plan it for ourselves, and bring all of you to make it more enjoyable.

**Liz**  Even Flo was saying how much she'd enjoyed it all.

**Kate**  Flo? But she finds something to grumble about in everything we do.

**Liz**  It's her way of being noticed.

**Kate**  We've had such wonderful weather — so little rain — but Flo still believes it should have waited until we got back.

**Liz**  Careful — here she comes. You'd think she'd heard us.

*Flo enters and collapses into a chair*

**Flo**  I'm looking for Freda.

**Kate**  Freda is looking for you.

**Flo**  Is she? I heard about the passport. Good old Freda — taking our minds off tomorrow's journey.

**Kate**  Now, Flo, you said you found the outward journey very interesting.

**Flo**  I did the history and all that. That was very nice. My brain enjoyed it — but it didn't reach my bottom. Where is Freda?

**Kate**  With Frau Klein arranging for Anton to take her to the police for a certificate she'll be needing. She wants you to go with her.

**Flo**  Of course I will.

**Liz**  You and Freda are good friends, aren't you?

**Flo**  Freda is a very nice person; a quality person. She treats everyone the same — with respect, and she's so clever. She's worth two of them who sometimes make fun of her.

**Kate**  No one makes fun of her, Flo. It's only gentle teasing.

**Flo**  Gentle or not,  they shouldn't. It's lack of respect. Shut up — here she comes.

*Freda enters slowly. She is out of breath*

**Freda**  Oh — there you are, Flo.

**Flo**  Sit down, Freda, for Heaven's sake, or you'll have a heart attack. I've heard all about the passport — and of course I'll come with you to the police. Though I don't expect I'll be much help.

**Freda**  You've taken a load off my mind. Frau Klein says they'll ask a lot of questions, and I know I'll get muddled. You've got such a wonderful, quick brain.

**Flo**  Me?

**Freda**  Yes, Flo. You can take my word about that. I've spent my life with other people's minds.

**Flo**  Well, well.

**Kate**  We're finishing off the wine. Will you have some?

**Flo**  No, thank you. I've had enough, and so has Freda.

**Freda**  I haven't.

**Flo**  All right then. Just a little.

*Kate pours out two glasses of wine and hands them over as they talk*

**Liz**  Is Frau Klein still with Anton?

**Flo**  Yes — in the bar.

**Liz**  Excuse me, please. I want a word with her.

*Elizabeth hurries out*

**Flo**  A bit sudden, wasn't it? You know, Kate — she's terribly upset about leaving.

**Kate**  We've talked, and I'm sure it helped. She's going to pass over the staff present tonight.

**Flo** Quite right. She's got such a lot out of this holiday. (*Pause*) Oh, Lord — peace is over. Lottie is on her way.

**Freda** Lottie is very kind. She helped me with my packing.

*Lottie enters. She carries a hold-all*

**Lottie** (*as she enters*) I've just waved to Liz. Can I grab her chair? (*She sits*) Abigail has gone to have another go at closing her case.

**Flo** I told her. She bought far too much stuff in that market. Scarves and aprons, even a dirndl skirt. The full Tyrolean rig-out.

**Kate** She'll never wear it. It looks lovely here — but how will it look, shopping in her village?

**Freda** She says she'll wear it on a bright, sunny day.

**Kate** She hasn't heard the British weather forecast.

**Lottie** What's the forecast for tomorow — for travelling?

**Kate** Rain, I'm afraid — but bright intervals.

**Lottie** How lucky we've been to have such glorious weather! Unbelievable. Two weeks of being able to laze in the sun, without the children.

**Flo** You must have a very good husband.

**Lottie** No. Friends take over from me.

**Kate** (*cutting in*) Rosa Klein told me that a weather forecast she once heard has become her recipe for living. "Expect sunshine — but take an umbrella".

**Lottie** I like that.

**Flo** Look — the sun on the mountains. They're turning all gold and rosy.

**Lottie** That's very artistic of you, Flo.

**Flo** I was going to say, Lottie, that it reminded me of the pink cotton-wool stuff I wore on my chest when I was a child. Used to stink to high heaven.

**Lottie** Before my time.

**Flo** (*after a pause*) Snow looks pretty like that. I didn't enjoy all that glaring white when we went up there in the coach. And I hated them dark forests — millions of gloomy old Christmas trees. They look horrible without decorations …

**Lottie** You'd need a lot of tinsel for one of those.

**Flo** I am quite aware of that — thank you, Lottie.

**Lottie** Sorry.

**Flo** I suppose it was you who told Alison that the little wooden shacks on the slopes are for skiing couples who fancy a bit of a romp.

**Lottie** I told her they are referred to locally as "hanky-panky huts".

**Flo** She believed you, and told everyone else.

**Freda** So what are they? The huts ?

**Kate** They store the hay — cattle food. Very necessary.

**Freda** That reminds me. Kate, about the journey, will you remind Harry to make as many stops as he can? Please.

**Kate** He always does. He can only stop at special parking-places or service stations.

**Lottie** I hate those service stations with a fierce German frau sitting by the door in the Ladies, ready to grab your money. Terrifying.

**Flo** Worse when there's one in the Men's.

**Lottie** One huge female grabbed hold of Bill Watson as he went in. Frightened him to death.

**Flo** Poor little Bill. That woman could have eat him.

**Kate** Don't worry, Freda — there will be plenty of stops.

**Flo** It's a pity bladders can't be left behind when you're travelling. Still, I wouldn't have missed them Austrian lavatories for anything. Spotless — beautiful tiles and shiny wood — every one a picture.

**Lottie** The holiday highlight for you, Flo? Austrian lavatories?

**Flo** Certainly. A great credit to them …

**Freda** Flo and I are not having service station food tomorrow, Kate. We've packed a picnic.

**Flo** I couldn't face them sausage things again. No wonder they label them —(*pronouncing the W*) *Wurst*. And I do know that's German for sausage, Lottie — and that they pronounce their W's like Vs. Stupid language.

**Kate** I wonder if Abigail has managed to close her case yet?

**Lottie** It's only the overnight one now. We were having a go at the big one when Hannah came along and offered to help. It was a riotous episode, but I don't think I ought to tell you about it.

**Flo** You will, Lottie, you will.

**Lottie** Hannah's a dear, but — well — she does look so very homely

— well — plain, doesn't she? And so deadly quiet. I mean — nothing. You just feel sorry for her.

**Kate**  Go on.

**Lottie**  I asked Hannah if her husband is meeting her. Just something to say. "He'll be there," she said. "I don't know how he's managed without me for two weeks." Abigail chipped in and said she'd filled her freezer with food, and I added "Me too." Then Hannah let the lid drop and said, "Oh, I don't mean *that*". Well, we kind of froze — then Abigail managed to say "You don't mean … ?" and stopped. Hannah gave us a beaming smile and said "Oh, yes — sex. Sometimes he comes home to lunch."

**Kate**  You're joking.

**Lottie**  Ask Abigail. Then Hannah shut the case, quite easily, and went out. I felt we should have genuflected.

**Kate**  Hannah — of all people!

**Lottie**  We must have looked damn stupid, just staring. A remarkable woman.

**Flo**  Well, I'm not a bit surprised. Hannah may not be a glamour puss, but she's real and comfortable. She's not a pathetic old has-been like Brenda — still chasing after the men.

**Kate**  We realize you don't approve of Brenda.

**Flo**  No, I don't. Did you see her the other night — at the folk evening? Showing off with the dancers — prancing around like a teenager on her National Health hips. Disgusting I call it at her age — specially when I reckon I've paid for them hips out of my Council Tax.

**Freda**  She has a right to enjoy herself, Flo. The same as you and me.

**Flo**  We don't make spectacles of ourselves.

**Freda**  Not in our own eyes. I know that people laugh at me sometimes.

**Flo**  Do you mind?

**Freda**  No. Neither, I'm sure, does Brenda. She just doesn't want to grow old.

**Lottie**  Of course not. Brenda hasn't finished with being young.

*Liz comes into view. She is hot and out of breath*

**Liz** Great excitement in the forecourt. The coach is back and Bill has got his angel. It's enormous — bigger than Dora. Huge and colourful.

**Lottie** Bill obviously likes big women.

**Kate** Where on earth is he going to put it? They live in a semi.

**Lottie** She'll have the guest room.

**Liz** Harry finally relented and said he'd somehow make room for her in the boot. There's been a lot of last-minute buying — getting rid of Austrian money. George and Joyce showed me their "souvenirs in sound". George bought a tape of church bells, and Joyce bought an ornamental cow-bell.

**Flo** They could have a coach-travel sound by clanking together some duty-free bottles.

*Kate shakes her head in disapproval*

**Kate** These shopping expeditions make me nervous. Do you remember, Lottie — a year or two ago, when Colin spent his left-over Deutschmarks on a scenic video for the coach journey home?

**Lottie** I'll never forget.

**Kate** When we put it on, it turned out to be the worst kind of porn.

**Lottie** I wish I had a picture of our faces. We had to dump the wretched video in a service station in case Colin was arrested by Customs. A pity — it was certainly scenic.

*There is laughter which dies away, and the women lapse into silence*

**Kate** It's still very warm. I'd go and have a shower if I didn't have to walk.

**Liz** No — don't go, Kate.

**Kate** Why, Liz — you sound very urgent.

**Liz** Frau Klein is coming to join us soon.

**Kate** Before dinner? I thought she'd be hawk-eyed in the kitchen.

*A glow from the setting sun has begun to creep slowly over the terrace*

**Freda** Look at the mountains, now. Breathtaking.
**Liz** I'll try and get a picture.
**Freda** You could never describe it, could you? It's too much.

*Liz moves a short distance away, focuses her camera and takes a picture. She then returns to the group*

**Liz** It's not only what we're seeing, is it? It's what we're feeling now — seeing it together, in this light.
**Kate** (*looking round*) We're beginning to glow — almost literally.
**Flo** Could be the wine.
**Kate** Of course. Wine warms the heart, and loosens the tongue. We're relaxed, comfortable — looking forward to this evening.

*There is a pause in the conversation*

**Freda** Happy. We're happy.
**Kate** I suppose so. I'm not sure. Is anyone totally happy — for long? Do we know when we're happy?
**Lottie** It goes by too quickly. You can't hold it.
**Freda** You know when you look back.

*There is another silence. The chattering gives way to slow, thoughtful speech*

**Liz** There are so many other words, aren't there?
**Kate** For what?
**Liz** Happiness. There's joy, ecstasy, delight.
**Freda** Contentment — bliss.
**Kate** Euphoria. All very different.
**Lottie** Elation — rapture. Some words last longer than others.
**Freda** Peace. Yes — peace.
**Flo** No, not peace. That's something you may not want. They put a wreath — "AT PEACE" — on my father's coffin. Rubbish. All he wanted was to live.
**Freda** Be quiet, Flo. You're spoiling it. Give us another word for happiness.

**Flo** I'm no good at words.

**Lottie** Oh, yes you are.

**Kate** Come on, Flo — you must know what it is to be happy.

**Flo** Yes.

**Kate** Tell us.

**Flo** I was a very happy child … There was me and my sister — and Ma and Pa. Specially Pa. He thought the world of me. My sister was very pretty. As we grew up people used to talk about us as the Reid sisters: the pretty Miss Reid — and the other one.

**Kate** Did you mind?

**Flo** Being "the other one"? Not as long as I had Pa. (*Pause*) When he died I went to one of them spirit meetings. The medium woman obligingly brought someone back for nearly everyone there — with a message from the "other side".

**Kate** What sort of messages?

**Flo** A bit like seaside postcards. "Having a lovely time." "Wish you were here." "See you soon." It was disgusting. The woman must have thought we were as batty as she was — and I told her so. There, out loud, at the meeting. It was chaos — and I was glad.

**Lottie** You are a very forthright person, Flo.

**Flo** I speak my mind.

**Lottie** That can be a very sad statement.

**Kate** (*cutting in*) What about you, Liz? How would you define happiness?

**Liz** I can give you a perfect example, from a few days ago. The chairlift — in sunshine — going to the top of the mountain. The silence — the tops of the trees waving to me — the wild flowers below — toy cattle. Finally, stepping into the snow. Ecstasy.

**Kate** For me the balconies, and the houses wrapped in flowers. What about you, Freda? Highlights?

**Freda** Salzburg — Mozart's house. And companionship.

*The colour in the sky is deepening. Lottie reaches for the hold-all and takes out a small camcorder*

**Lottie** I know I shall regret not having pictures when I'm boasting to my friends. This is supposed to be a good camcorder, but I don't know how to use the beastly thing.

**Liz** Can I help?

**Lottie** Would you? Can we take some pictures from the balcony?

**Liz** Of course.

**Freda** I'll come too. All gadgets hate me, but I'd like to learn. Are you coming, Flo?

**Flo** No — I'm comfortable. I'll record it in my mind.

*Lottie, Liz, and Freda exit*

**Flo** (*breaking into the silence*) It's good to see you having a bit of a rest.

**Kate** It's a long journey tomorrow — and a hundred things to see to in the morning.

**Flo** Bound to be.

**Kate** Will you do something for me, Flo?

**Flo** Of course

**Kate** Harry told me we're getting short of coffee on the coach. In the morning, will you pick up some I've ordered from Frau Klein?

**Flo** With pleasure.

**Kate** And pass it on to Lottie?

**Flo** (*after a pause*) I'll ask Liz.

**Kate** Why not you?

**Flo** I look after Freda.

**Kate** We all do that — and Freda is not helpless.

**Flo** Liz gets on with Lottie better than I do.

**Kate** Why, Flo ... Why don't you get on with Lottie? Everyone else does.

**Flo** I don't dislike her. I know she means well.

**Kate** Damning by faint praise.

**Flo** She teases Freda.

**Kate** That's petty. Freda is always singing Lottie's praises. Come on, Flo, out with it. What's the real reason?

**Flo** We're very different people.

**Kate** You're two of a kind — that's the problem.

**Flo** Lottie belongs to what my Pa used to call "the useless class".

**Kate** So she chose her family, did she? That's racism, Flo — as bad as black and white, or any other.

**Flo**  That's ridiculous.

**Kate**  That's the truth. I can speak my mind too.

**Flo**  All right. I've got nothing in common with someone like Lottie. I'm surprised she comes away with a mixed bunch like us. Like my Pa, I've never had time for people who go through the world the easy way.

**Kate**  And that includes Lottie?

**Flo**  She's well-off — too much money to fling around. Spoiled I reckon, probably all her life.

**Kate**  And that irritates you?

**Flo**  I suppose so.

**Kate**  Envy?

**Flo**  No. (*Pause*) Perhaps. Not for myself — I've been lucky. For others who haven't.

**Kate**  What did you make of Lottie's reply to you — about her husband and the children?

**Flo**  That she's a widow. Or did he leave her?

**Kate**  Lottie is not a widow. (*She pauses*) Flo — I'm going to break a promise I've kept for several years. Will you give me your solemn word not to pass on anything of what I'm going to tell you?

**Flo**  You can trust me.

**Kate**  I know. Lottie is not a widow, that would have been much easier for her.

**Flo**  She's got children.

**Kate**  She has one — a son. Nicky is fourteen now. When Nicky was four, Lottie's husband left her.

**Flo**  For someone else?

**Kate**  Not at the time. He left her because of the boy. Nicky is physically handicapped — severely — and autistic. Lottie's husband left because she wouldn't put Nicky in a home.

**Flo**  Poor little soul.

**Kate**  They divorced, and he remarried — a well-known name often in the news. He can afford that kind of wife and still be generous to Lottie.

**Flo**  Has she still got the boy?

**Kate**  Yes. And three other rejects she's bringing up with Nicky.

**Flo**  Three! Handicapped?

**Kate**  And autistic, which is worse. Lottie's house is miles from anywhere, which is just as well. Being there with the children is like being in a zoo.

*There is silence*

**Kate**  She has good helpers who can take over — but the final scene is Lottie's.
**Flo**  Year in; year out.
**Kate**  Yes.
**Flo**  Sounds like hell. How does she bear it? Whatever can she get out of a life like that?
**Kate**  Challenge; excitement; purpose. Now and then a little progress.
**Flo**  That can't be enough.
**Kate**  It seems to be, for Lottie. Look at her, Flo — she's no martyr. Lively, fun-loving, energetic. She's enjoying life, wouldn't you say?

*There is no answer*

Well?
**Flo**  So I was wrong, and I'm sorry. I wish I could say something to her — and I can't, can I?
**Kate**  It would be an awful thing to do — as you know. And the end of her trust in me.
**Flo**  I can try not to argue with her.
**Kate**  No, for Heaven's sake! She'd suspect something. Anyway, she likes you as you are.
**Flo**  And what am I?
**Kate**  You're two people standing side by side. Caring Flo with Freda — stubborn Flo with Lottie.
**Flo**  Two people.
**Kate**  Most of us are.
**Flo**  Stubborn. (*She shakes her head*). I can see that in other people, and I suppose they can see it in me. Why can't I see it in myself?
**Kate**  We just cannot — "see ourselves as others see us!" Famous words, Flo.

**Flo**  Who wrote them?

**Kate**  A poet. Robert Burns.

**Flo**  A living poet?

**Kate**  Sort of.

**Flo**  Does anyone else on the tour know about Lottie?

**Kate**  Some may know she's bringing up a family on her own. That's all. Be careful — they're coming back. Don't forget your promise — ever. And don't look tragic,because it's not. Smile.

*Lottie, Liz and Freda stroll in, and gradually get seated again*

**Lottie**  I hope the film comes out. There's a wonderful view from the balcony. Liz took the pictures — this thing is too elaborate for me.

**Liz**  It's a superb camcorder, and it isn't really difficult.

**Lottie**  Not for you.

**Liz**  It's all in the instructions. You could have a lovely record of your children as they grow up.

**Flo**  (*cutting in*) I'm like Lottie — no good with gadgets. My microwave blew up the first time I used it.

*They are slightly surprised at the outburst*

**Lottie**  Bad luck.

**Freda**  I wish I could paint a sky like that. I have tried.

**Flo**  I didn't know you did painting.

**Freda**  I'm not very good

**Flo**  It's something I've always wanted to try. It's too late now.

**Kate**  Nonsense. Come to the college on a beginner's course. You and Freda.

**Flo**  That's quite an idea. What about it, Freda? Worth thinking over?

**Freda**  A wonderful idea. Something to look forward to.

*There is silence again as they watch the mountains*

*Frau Klein enters unobtrusively*

**Frau Klein**  In this light you look like a group of statues.

**Kate**  We've been hypnotized by the mountains. What a sky!

**Frau Klein**  Putting on a show for your last evening.

**Kate**  Will you have a drink, now?

**Frau Klein**  Thank you — I will now.

**Kate**  You should have come out earlier. We've been discussing happiness.

**Frau Klein**  A solemn subject surely — for after a party? Did you make any discoveries?

**Kate**  Not really.

**Lottie**  I wouldn't say that. We agreed that we spend our lives searching for happiness, without knowing what it is.

**Liz**  Or without recognizing it when we find it.

**Frau Klein**  Was it your idea, Elizabeth — discussing happiness?

**Liz**  I just talked about the chairlift.

**Frau Klein**  Oh.

**Liz**  I've been waiting until you joined us …

*There is some surprise and anticipation as they all turn to look at Liz. Liz has to make an effort to begin speaking*

Now that Frau Klein is here, I have something very special to say which I know is going to be a great surprise — especially to Kate. Perhaps a shock, and I apologize for that. (*She pauses to breathe deeply*) I shall not be going back with you tomorrow. Probably not for a long while.

*There is a general reaction of extreme surprise*

**Kate**  Liz! What are you saying?!

**Liz**  I'm staying in Austria. Ever since that first hour here the idea has been creeping into my mind — and of course I pushed it away. It was so crazy — impossible. Then — several days ago, while I was talking to Frau Klein — she told me that Maria is soon leaving to get married — and she offered me a job in the hotel. A three month try-out for both of us. I refused at once — it was unthinkable.

**Kate**  And now?

**Liz**  Suddenly the way seems perfectly clear.

**Kate**  But why — so suddenly?

**Liz**  I'm not sure. Perhaps it was the party — perhaps it was you, Kate — reminding me how, "Time is slipping underneath our feet".

**Kate**  Liz — I can't find words.

**Liz**  I'm really sorry, Kate, about the shock.

**Kate**  I feel responsible — and a bit shaken by all that it means. And that's ridiculous, because it's wonderful of course.

**Lottie**  It's fantastic. Unbelievable. I know you'll look back on this as the greatest day of your life.

**Freda**  And the bravest.

**Liz**  Not brave enough to go home and face the rows. Mother, and Laura, and Tony — a mountain of arguments. I shall telephone them tonight, and from then on they'll have to cope because I won't be there.

**Kate**  Well, Rosa, you seem to have had a leading part in this.

**Frau Klein**  A tiny part as an arm of Fate, with Maria leaving so soon. I'd already interviewed several people for the job, but none of them were suitable. Maria speaks fluent English, and deals with all our British guests.

**Kate**  And Liz?

**Frau Klein**  Elizabeth is ideal. Her German is quite good, and will soon improve with practise.

**Kate**  But there's more to this than language, isn't there, Rosa? There's life itself.

**Frau Klein**  Elizabeth's life — and my responsibility. Believe me, Kate, I've had many hard years since Andreas died to learn to trust my own judgement, and intuition. I liked Elizabeth immediately. She will do well, and be happy I'm sure.

**Kate**  Any official problems?

**Frau Klein**  A routine process, that's all.

**Freda**  It's wonderful, Liz. You'll have so many memories for when you're old — and that's important.

*Kate starts to make a move*

**Kate** You know I'm really quite dazed. All this happening — and the wine.

**Frau Klein** Don't forget the hotel's farewell toast tonight.

**Kate** Unforgettable. Every year.

**Lottie** I shall drink a special toast tonight. To all crazy dreamers — like Bill and his angel.

**Klein** I must go. Angels won't serve your dinner — and neither will my staff until I'm there. Do you want me to delay it a bit?

**Kate** Don't worry, Rosa — we'll be there to do it full justice. A real celebration.

*Frau Klein hurries out*

*Freda makes a move*

**Freda** Come on, Flo, there's not much time. And I'm no good at hurrying, as you know.

**Flo** I do, Freda — I do.

*Freda and Flo exit*

*Lottie is about to follow, but is stopped by Kate*

**Kate** Lottie dear — I suggest we let Liz break her news to the rest.

**Lottie** Of course. Now am I likely to tell anyone?

**Kate** Yes.

**Lottie** You're right. I promise. My lips are sealed.

*Lottie exits*

**Liz** Telling everyone won't be difficult now that you know, Kate. That worried me. I wondered if I should have waited to tell you on your own.

**Kate** I think this was the best way. Why not give your news after handing over the staff present?

**Liz** Just what I was thinking.

**Kate** Before we go — you will keep in touch, won't you? From here. Regard us as a support system.

**Liz** That's a very comforting thought.

*They prepare to leave the terrace*

**Kate** You know, Liz — I think I shall have a feeling of elation as we cross the border tomorrow. What about you — waving goodbye?

**Liz** No tears. Not then anyway. Perhaps a few quiet ones later, as the excitement dies down. Thank goodness there will be so much practical stuff to do. As a priority, I must work on my German.

**Kate** And clothes shopping, full Tyrolean costume in the hotel. Gorgeous — lucky old you.

**Liz** I can't really grasp it all yet. Imagine the Austrian me waiting to greet your tour next year. (*She automatically starts to gather up bottles and glasses*)

**Kate** Don't start your job yet. Trudi will clear up later.

**Liz** I think I'll keep a bottle as a souvenir.

**Kate** Then take this one — it's half full. Drink a toast to us in Germany tomorrow night.

**Liz** I will. What time will you reach Boppard?

**Kate** At about six o'clock.

**Liz** So — at eight o'clock I'll raise a glass to you all.

**Kate** Eight o'clock.

**Liz** Don't forget.

**Kate** I promise.

*As they prepare to leave there is a distant clap of thunder, stopping them in their tracks*

**Kate** Thunder! There's a storm coming. See — lightning over there.

**Liz** The end of the heat wave.

**Kate** The first of many changes for you, Liz. Scared?

**Liz** No. I knew there may be thunder.

*There is another distant clap of thunder as they continue towards the hotel*

CURTAIN

# FURNITURE AND PROPERTY LIST

*On stage*:    Flowers
                  Small garden tables. *On one table*: bottles of wine; glasses
                  Garden chairs
                  Sun-lounger chairs
                  One full glass of wine for **Kate**

*Off stage*:    Hold-all containing small camcorder (**Lottie**)

*Personal*:    **Elizabeth:** camera
                  **Frau Klein**: ornate parcel

# LIGHTING PLOT

Practical fittings required: nil

*To open*: exterior warm, bright sunny light; late afternoon

| | | |
|---|---|---|
| *Cue* 1 | **Kate**: " ... hawk-eyed in the kitchen." | (Page 13) |
| | *Fade bright sunny effect slowly through play* | |
| | *to sunset effect. Bring up glow across terrace* | |
| | | |
| *Cue* 2 | **Freda**: "And companionship." | (Page 15) |
| | *Deepen sunset colour* | |

# EFFECTS PLOT

*Cue* 1     **Kate**: "I promise."        (Page 23)
*Sound of distant clap of thunder*

*Cue* 2     **Liz**: "I knew there may be thunder."        (Page 23)
*Sound of distant clap of thunder*